UNDER HIS SHADOW
WRITINGS
Volume 4

by David Mayorga

Published by

SHABAR PUBLICATIONS
www.shabarpublications.com

Most Shabar Publications products are available at special quantity discounts for bulk purchase for sales promotions, fund-raising and educational needs. For details, write Shabar Publications at mayorga1126@gmail.com.

Under His Shadow Writings Volume 4 *by David Mayorga*
Published by Shabar Publications
3833 N. Taylor Rd.
Palmhurst, Texas 78573
www.shabarpublications.com
www.masterbuildertx.com

ISBN 978-1-955433-18-1

Table of Contents

Introduction

Once again, my longing to pursue God's heart continues to burn with a deep passion and desire. Is there anything for a servant of God to do?

In the following 40 chapters of this book, you will find some great truths that God has been speaking to my heart. I intend you to be blessed and enriched by these writings, as they were all birthed in God's heart. I trust your heart will be set on fire as you fast and pray through these biblical truths!

I always recommend you find a good place, preferably quiet, to meet God daily. You might want to take this volume of notes, a pen or pencil, a journal, and the Bible. Get your heart quiet and listen to His voice. Write it down and be changed by His lovely voice!

Because He loved me first,
David Mayorga, *Author*

Day 1
Are You Willing to be Searched by God?

"Search me [thoroughly], O God, and know my heart! Try me and know my thoughts! And see if there is any wicked or hurtful way in me and lead me in the way everlasting." (Psalm 139:23, 24 Amplified Version)

In opening this deep thought of how the Psalmist prayed as he said, "**Search me** [thoroughly], **O God, and know my heart,** one can only ponder the attitude of a man who has nothing to hide before His Maker.

The Psalmist's prayer interests me because he longs to be cleansed from all malice. He doesn't want anything to be between him and the Lord. Where does one learn this? How do you get to thinking this way? I believe this can only happen as the Spirit of the Lord moves in you and me. This crying out to God can only be given by invitation from the Holy Spirit to a deeper life in God.

I believe that as we draw near to the Lord, this prayer becomes more intense and more accurate, especially for him who longs to be right with God, for that person who desires that there be no gulf between God and himself. What contriteness of our heart and will. If there is something we must learn, it is to hear the promptings of the Holy Spirit as He whispers His wishes to us for a deeper, more intimate relationship with Him.

The Psalmist continues to press into the heart of the matter as he invites the Lord to look inside. How many of us allow God to look inside our hearts? Have you taken the time to let this happen to you? I don't think it is easy to do this, but those who long to be more like Jesus will do this continually. This is indeed a mark of spiritual growth and maturity.

Now, what exactly is the Psalmist asking God to do? He asks the Lord to search him for two specific things: 1) in his thoughts and 2) if there might be any wicked or hurtful way deep within his heart.

The thoughts speak of disquieting thoughts (caused by secrets kept); and wicked is translated pain. In other words, have you been hurt and are now carrying pain? It is a serious matter because wherever pain goes, it will cause pain. So healing is needed. Do you understand this?

Under His Shadow Prayer

"Holy Spirit, go deep into my heart and align it with Yours. I want to be free from guilt and shame, so please forgive me for keeping ungodly secrets and for allowing my heart to become wicked due to the pain that I received from someone or something. Forgive me for the people I have offended with my words, attitudes, and actions. Holy Spirit, don't let anything pass without you "checking it at the door." Search me deep and cleanse me with the blood of Jesus and perfect me in holiness." Amen.

Day 2
The Need for a New Heart!

"Create in me a clean heart, O God,
And renew a steadfast spirit within me.
Do not cast me away from Your presence,
And do not take Your Holy Spirit from me."
(Psalm 51:10-11)

This morning, as I pondered the heart of the Lord, my spirit jumped with joy and expectation when I heard King David's heart as he penned this wonderful Psalm 51. If you have read it in depth, it speaks of David's confession to adultery and murder.

Without a doubt, this must be one of David's lowest points in his life, and his notes have been left for all of us: a manual to walk through the wilderness of unworthiness due to self and sin.

After David confesses before the Prophet Nathan, he cries out to the Lord out of the anguish of his own heart and repents wholeheartedly before God.

You see, before this colossal failure, David, the king of Israel, had everything at his disposal. Anything he wished or desired, he would quickly get. For some reason, David didn't do this. David saw this beautiful woman and didn't settle for the conviction of the Holy Spirit in his heart. David brought her into his chambers and impregnated her. He didn't know what to do when the matter was found out. So he brought the husband in from battle so that he would sleep with his wife, but he didn't. He felt a disloyalty toward David to sleep with his wife while the army of Israel was in battle. After David's attempt to get the man to sleep with his wife failed, David had the man put on the front lines so he might be killed in battle. In this way, David hid his sins. Nobody knew it, but God knew it.

After a while, the matter was revealed to the Prophet Nathan, who later confronted David with this secret sin. David was heartbroken and contrite before the Prophet and before God.

True Repentance

David knew he had transgressed and crossed the line with

his sins. He knew that nobody deserved to get hurt by this, but his sinful nature took over, and David failed miserably.

Around this time, David comes clean before God and pleads with God for forgiveness of his sins. His prayer was sincere and heartfelt, and the Lord heard it.

Now, David had a deep prayer request before God. He touched God's heart and said, "Create a clean heart, oh God, and renew a steadfast spirit within me. "

David's first cry was that God would create a new heart in him, asking God to shape his heart again to its original form. He also added that God would renew (which means repair in Hebrew) a steadfast [firm] spirit within him.

David adds another portion to his prayer and asks the Lord, **"Do not cast me away from Your presence, and do not take Your Holy Spirit from me."** David knows the value of God's presence and doesn't want to live a day without it or away from Him. He never wants to be apart from the Holy Spirit – ever!

Under His Shadow Prayer

"*Precious Holy Spirit, take me deeper into Your heart and help me to see what you see, to feel what you feel, and break my heart with the things that break Yours. Don't ever let me go from your presence! Repair me, repair me, repair me, Oh God!*" Amen.

Day 3
Fan Into Flames!

"For this reason, I am reminding you to fan into flames the gift of God that is within you through the laying on of my hands." (2 Timothy 1:6)

In our walk with God, the servant of the Lord will soon realize that his salvation didn't cost him anything. His salvation was paid in full by Jesus Christ. All one must do is enter into it by faith. All one must do is accept God's free gift of divine life, and one will experience God's anointing.

The proper way to enter is to confess with the mouth and believe with the heart that Jesus is Lord. Christ's beautiful work upon the cross of Calvary is God's free gift of salvation to anyone who calls out to Him from a pure heart.

Now, the walk with Christ is an altogether different story. It is not free but costly. Very costly. To enter the life of Christ by faith is one thing, but to discipline oneself to follow Christ step by step is the real challenge for any would-be follower of Jesus.

The devil, the flesh, and the world are all aligned and ready to make their move in quenching your God-given ambitions and desires.

If you haven't realized it yet, the walk of faith in Christ has its challenges and battles.

When one decides to please God, they will wake up on a battlefield. As God's servant opens his eyes in the early morning, he will be met with solid forces arrayed against him. Some are more subtle than others; nevertheless, its effect is the same: to quench the fire of God in you!

As discouraged and disillusioned as you may become due to your various challenges, you must get up and shake yourself. You are to put on the whole armor of God and make your way to the battlefield. You must discipline your body so that at the end of your life, you don't end up being disqualified.

The servant must also note that you cannot have someone else fanning the flame inside you; you must be the one to do it!

This is what it means to 'fan into flames,' the gift that God has given you. Don't let the flickering flame (as small as it may seem) go out! Never let it go out!

Under His Shadow Prayer

"Dear Holy Spirit and friend, I yield my flesh to your Spirit this morning. I ask you for strength to arise and to dress for battle with Your armor. I need Your touch this morning; yes, the anointing that breaks the yoke, the covering of the blood that washed away my guilty stains, and the courage to get up and continue showing up to battle. Jesus, my heart longs to please You in all things. Work in me and bring ever so close to Your heart!" Amen.

Day 4
Make Me an Instrument!

Therefore, do not let sin reign in your mortal body, that you should obey it in its lusts. And do not present your members as instruments of unrighteousness to sin but present yourselves to God as being alive from the dead, and your members as instruments of righteousness to God." (Romans 6:12, 13)

The highest honor and calling for anyone created by God is to do and live out the purpose for what they were created. Anything else that we live out between this understanding is only coincidental. We must live to be God's vessels and holy instruments.

Can you imagine the Master taking you or me as an instrument into His hands? If it's a valuable vase to put flowers in, an instrument to make music, or any other instrument with a purpose, the touch of His hands as He handles it, the tenderness and cautiousness with which He would handle such a thing of value- the thought of Him handling with His own hands an instrument He created for His good pleasure - to see this would be priceless to me.

But What About the Instrument?

In Romans 6, the Bible calls you and I instruments. We could be instruments of unrighteousness if we allow ourselves to be directed by the flesh and its works, or we can be called instruments of righteousness for His use alone.

The challenge we have before us is not knowing that the flesh is an enemy of Christ, but when tempted by it, can we overcome it by Christ's power? Can we remain in constant purity before God as temptation pours on us? Will we stay pure for His use? When the time comes when God needs an instrument for His use, will we be ready? Will we be a pure vessel that He can pour Himself into? Our challenge is to stay pure before Him!

In my early years as a believer, as I learned to walk in His kingdom, our church would sing this chorus on Sunday morning gatherings. The lyrics to this one song were so embedded in my heart as the worship leader would take us before the throne and position us for such glorious encounters with our King...

Lord make me an instrument,
An instrument of worship.
I lift up my hands in Your Name.
Lord make me an instrument,
An instrument of worship.
I lift up my hands in Your Name.

Lord, tune me, Your instrument,
An instrument of worship.
I lift my hands in Your Name.
Lord, tune me Your instrument,
An instrument of worship.
I lift my hands in Your Name. [Author Unknown]

Under His Shadow Prayer

"King Jesus, don't ever pass me by. I desire to be your instrument of righteousness. Continually fine-tune my life; speak to my heart daily and teach me Your ways. May I find favor in Your eyes, and when You need a vessel, yes, an instrument - that I would be so tuned up and ready that You don't pass me by! Place Your lovely hands upon me and use me for Your honor and glory, Jesus!" Amen.

Day 5
It's Time to Fix What is Broken!

"Then I said to them, "You see the distress that we are in, how Jerusalem lies waste, and its gates are burned with fire. Come and let us build the wall of Jerusalem, that we may no longer be a reproach." (Nehemiah 2:17)

As I sought the Lord this early morning, I envisioned this tall wall surrounding the city. It was a big wall, but interestingly, the Lord set my eyes on a portion of that wall. The wall seemed complete from afar, but I realized the top portion was broken as I focused more on it.

This is precisely what happens in our lives – we are too in a hurry from one place to another that we don't see the breaking happening. Unless we focus on it, we won't see it.

Now, from where I was standing, I could see the wall. I noticed that it was broken at the top. The whole wall was intact except for a tiny portion at the top. I couldn't leave it alone, so I set myself to fix it.

Here's what I believe the Lord spoke to my heart:

David, the wall is complete and intact. Yet, there are areas in the wall that need to be fixed. I have given you an eye for perfection, and what you see is what you must change by fixing it! End of vision.

In the abovementioned story, Nehemiah was God's man for the hour. God raised him to come to Jerusalem and evaluate how badly the walls had been damaged. The Lord desired to fix the walls but needed a man to act and do something about it – Nehemiah was that man!

Section by section, Nehemiah rallied the men around him to fix every bit of it, not to mention they did this amid opposition. A few men didn't want the honor of Jerusalem restored. So, they opposed Nehemiah in the reconstruction of the city walls.

We must always note that the enemy will ensure it doesn't go as planned in rebuilding for God's honor and glory. He will fight, intimidate, try to send you away, and stop building.

The word for this morning is: Look around for any broken sections of the wall in your own life. When you find them, fix them. No matter what the enemy says, fix them! All for the beauty of His house!

Under His Shadow Prayer

"Lord Jesus, as I ponder this truth in my heart, please help me see the areas of my life that are broken, in need of repair, or must be replaced. I don't want to live a life with broken walls. I want to bring glory and honor to Your spiritual temple. Please forgive me for my carelessness in keeping the walls looking nice and presentable before You. Restore the desire to be attentive to this temple, Your house, Oh Lord." Amen.

Day 6
Perfect Me in Holiness Oh God!

"Having therefore these promises, dearly beloved, let us cleanse ourselves from all filthiness of the flesh and spirit, perfecting holiness in the fear of God." (2 Corinthians 7:1)

When Christ, our Lord, called us out of sin, He called us out to Himself. He didn't call us out to the work of ministry, as some may suppose; He called us out to be like Him, walk like Him, and act like Him. When the Holy Spirit touched our lives, it was to serve Him and be made in His image.

Often, believers feel that now that they are saved, they feel called to win souls, help the local church, and do social work. At least, this is what pastors tell their congregants. Though coming to Christ and becoming a follower of Him is a great idea, the high calling truly is to be more and more like Him in character, word, and deed.

In many Christian circles, pastors feel that creating vast networks, building more prominent buildings, or extending their campuses to the four corners of their region is all part of God's plan. I venture to say that these people are dealing with some ego issues!

When Christ died for you and me, He died so we could love Him, become like Him, and serve Him.

Now, I believe God has His people in touch with Him who are called to do extensive outreach, to plant churches in places where there is no church, or to launch a ministry that will cause an impact on the lost. I get this type of vision. What I find hard to understand is how, today, everyone has an itch to become somebody big in ministry.

Getting Back to the Basics...

In my prayer time today, I realized that God has called you and me to be holy people, perfect in holiness in the fear of the Lord! Holiness means separating oneself from the Lord. It also means a purity of heart birthed out of the fear of the Lord.

The first call is to have a pure heart before God. Then, anything that God might reveal to this this type of heart. Anything else regarding ministry opportunities must follow a pure heart – not the other way around.

Paul's words, when he says, **"Let us cleanse ourselves from all filthiness of the flesh and spirit..."** Paul is calling God's servants to a responsibility. The responsibility is a personal cleansing from all filthiness of the flesh and spirit. What does this mean?

This verse means that we, as God's servants, are called to cleanse ourselves from all forms of filth. Filth here is a heresy, a following of a pagan way of life. It is allowing oneself to be part of a pagan lifestyle.

That is what believers have adopted into their lives today – a pagan lifestyle. You see it on social media, you see it on worldly outlets of information, and you see it on the lukewarm believer's lifestyle. It is everywhere in the land today.

Preachers have given themselves almost entirely to these practices and accept them as culturally relevant. I call it compromising the truth of God's divine order.

The church is missing something, and it is not new songs and sounds; it is not more theological perspectives or end-time revelations; it is missing the anointing of God. The church is powerless, purposeless, and void of His presence. Help, Lord, for the godly man ceases from the land!

Under His Shadow Prayer

"Dear Jesus, help me become a man who seeks Your face amid this dark and apathetic world of Christianity that has been created. I pray you would stir me to set ablaze everyone I encounter –clergy or a humble disciple." Amen.

Day 7
Many Voices!

"For the weapons of our warfare are not physical [weapons of flesh and blood], but they are mighty before God for the overthrow and destruction of strongholds, [Inasmuch as we] refute arguments and theories and reasonings and every proud and lofty thing that sets itself up against the [true] knowledge of God; and we lead every thought and purpose away captive into the obedience of Christ (the Messiah, the Anointed One)." (2 Corinthians 10:4, 5 Amplified Version)

As we press forward as God's vessels and soldiers of the cross of Christ, there will be days when the enemy will come in and flood you with vain arguments in your mind.

Vicious arguments contrary to God's plan for your life will increase. Reasonings that challenge your position as a believer will also try to overthrow you from the faith. These are very real!

As I continue my prayer and fasting journey, I have dealt with prophetic dreams that are not so positive. They are complex and with an undertone of negativity.

As my dreams end, I hear a slightly quiet voice that says, I am going to destroy you; I am going to take everything away from you. You will not survive! Words of this nature have been bombarding my mind in the last few days; obviously, these are not words from the Lord!

The minute you and I decide to advance in God's call or pursuit of His knowledge, all hell will break loose! Mark it down.

The enemy knows what we can become if we discover the ways of the Lord. He knows that we will become a weapon in the hands of a holy God. The enemy cannot afford this and will do all he can to deter us, whether in thought or deed.

In the Scripture above, Paul says that we have the power to destroy strongholds, which are fortified structures or prisons that make every effort to keep us believing something mentally. Paul also adds that God can deliver us from vain arguments and reasonings, which speak of thoughts that challenge the very essence of who we are in God.

To all these attacks of the mind, the Lord has made provision in the finished work of Christ. We can take every thought captive to the obedience of Christ!

The next time you hear a negative report in your mind, know it has come to challenge what you believe God to be and do! Amen.

Under His Shadow Prayer

"Lord Jesus, my King and Lord, nothing is more powerful than you. Though the enemy rages and makes every effort to make me change my mind about You, what You have done for me, and who I am in You, I will continue to press into You. You promised that nothing or no one can take me away from the palm of Your hand. I believe you, Jesus!" Amen.

Day 8
The Real Challenge!

"And although you were at one time estranged and alienated and hostile-minded [toward Him], participating in evil things, yet Christ has now reconciled you [to God] in His physical body through death, in order to present you before the Father holy and blameless and beyond reproach-- [and He will do this] if you continue in the faith, well-grounded and steadfast, and not shifting away from the [confident] hope [that is a result] of the gospel that you have heard, which was proclaimed in all creation under heaven, and of which [gospel] I, Paul, was made a minister." (Colossian 1:22-23 Amplified Version)

When we think of a challenge, we usually get a picture of someone crossing a barrier, climbing a mountain cliff and attempting to reach the summit, or finishing an extensive obstacle course. Though these challenges work wonders for someone's mindset, let us look at the definition of the word challenge.

In *Oxford's Learners Dictionary*, a *challenge* is a new or difficult task that tests someone's ability and skill.

As you probably have learned, challenges come in various forms and sizes. The goal is to overcome them, get to the other side, and live to tell how one did it. Every challenge is designed to make one better, not bitter!

Also, as you have already experienced, every skill and every form of ability is displayed; only those who tap into their skill overcome. Challenges have been designed for character formation with the result of developing a better man or woman.

Being Challenged in the Spirit!

After one has been reconciled to God through the blood of Christ, that man or woman will be challenged in his or her faith. You and I will be challenged multiple times in our faith, and it (our faith) will be purified as by fire, the Scripture says. [See 1 Peter 1:7].

In the natural, one discovers how strong or weak mentally, emotionally, and physically they are as they try to overcome their present challenge. In the spiritual aspect, one is tested in the spiritual side, mainly in how solid and real their faith is. As a side note, one must know that our faith is only as strong as our last challenge.

There are many promises to those who follow Christ in the spirit, not the flesh. If one overcomes by growing more profoundly in the knowledge of Christ, instead of giving in to the desires of the flesh, one will be transformed more like Christ. This is the goal – to be more like Christ.

Whenever you and I face a challenge, our faith is under probation. Will we remain in Christ, grow, or yield to the flesh and lose ground? Will we surrender to our lower nature or tap into Christ's power?

Under His Shadow Prayer

"Lord Jesus, help me as my life is bombarded with challenges; some challenges are so strong that I need more of You. Please help me see these challenges forming before they come and run over me. My prayer is simple: Jesus, "Keep me in a mode of warfare always!" Amen.

Day 9
Encounters of the God Kind!

"And Enoch walked with God; and he was not, for God took him." (Genesis 5:24)

This morning, during my quiet time, I began to feel the need to ascend to God's throne and to come before Him with a humble heart, to ask Him for help in my own life, and to lead me accordingly.

In pondering the life of Enoch here in Genesis 5, I was stirred in my heart by this man's desire to walk with God. It doesn't say a whole lot about the life of Enoch, but one thing is clear – Enoch walked with God!

Is there a need to know anything more?

The Scripture says, "And he was not, for God took him."

God Encounters

In my short life before God, I have had some mind-boggling experiences; they were hard to explain and describe and, indeed, supernatural. Yet, I was never taken away to any place; in my mind, I wasn't. Now, Enoch was taken by the Lord to be with Him!

Now, what does this entail? I don't know. It is sufficient to say that I have been taken to various places in the Spirit but have always been brought back to my original spot. My heart and mind were carried to other countries for times of intercession but then brought back to the place where I was. It's extraordinary if you ask me.

I do believe that God does draw His servants near to His heart for seasons of encounters. I'm not saying this happens to all, but it could; I'm not saying this happens all the time. I'm saying that God can carry us away anywhere He wishes. You can call it an ascension, a rapture of sorts, or you can enjoy the ride and tell others about your experience with God.

I was recently taken in the spirit of the country of Venezuela. Please don't ask me why I got there or was taken there because I don't know. What I do know is this: God took me and placed me in the middle of a worship team that was praying in a circle on a church stage and began interceding for a move of God in their country. I was so broken and caught up in this glorious moment with loud moaning that when I was awakening, I was still in the spirit of this event! Go figure.

I thanked God for taking me there and allowing me to experience this type of intercession. I know God moves in these ways and desire to see more of it.

Under His Shadow Prayer

"Jesus, thank you for your Spirit that moves in and around us. Thank you that you desire for Your people to soar like eagles and be in touch with You. May I always be ready to pray and intercede for world events and churches (both local and global). Help me always to stay in sync with Your will and Spirit." Amen.

Day 10
Discerning Direction!

"Now when Herod was dead, behold, an angel of the Lord appeared in a dream to Joseph in Egypt, saying, "Arise, take the young Child and His mother, and go to the land of Israel, for those who sought the young Child's life are dead." (Matthew 2:19-20)

When seeking direction for your life, the believer has the most advanced compass ever created for humanity: his Word, His Spirit, and God's Angelic messengers. The exciting thing about these three methods is that they always align. They are never opposites and never in conflict with each other!

Discerning God's will for our lives has always been done similarly. As profound and intense the inner witness in our hearts may be, it should always align with God's Word.

In our world, you must always be mindful that there are many voices today; every voice has a specific significance.

One is to glorify flesh, and others glorify God. It would be best if you learned to discern the difference.

The servant of the Lord must always be attentive to the potential of emotional misleading. Many things sound good and look good, but they are not the Lord's will for you. Just because you like it and prefer it to be that way doesn't mean God feels the same about your observation. Please note that the witness is in the Spirit, not your flesh. One must learn to discern the difference.

Use Inward Peace as a Signpost!

Using peace to dictate what you feel inside is an excellent tell-tell sign that God may lead you in the way. If, when a decision is about to be made, you feel troubled inside yourself and don't want to make that turn, it is probably God telling you that you are about to make a wrong decision.

You see, often, our hearts may feel troubled by a choice we are about to make, but our spirit feels a deep, subtle peace that this is the way, then one must trust God by faith.

My counsel to anyone is to constantly learn to listen and experience the subtle peace of God as they follow His will.

Angels in Dreams!

In the Scripture above, Joseph had a spiritual experience where an angel appeared to him in a dream. In this prophetic dream, the angel told him to return to Israel. Notice the details: an angel had initially told him some time back to go to Egypt, for Herod would try to kill Jesus – so Joseph and his wife fled to Egypt. Now, it was time to come back to Israel.

I do believe that God sometimes leads us this way. He will bring us into something we must be aware of, then take us out of that place. Be on the lookout for God's prophetic leadership ways.

Under His Shadow Prayer

"Jesus, lead me by Your Word, Spirit, and heavenly messengers. Help me to discern Your voice and feel Your deep, subtle peace throughout my life!" Amen.

Day 11
God's Perspective!

"But Noah found grace in the eyes of the Lord." (Genesis 6:8)

As the world began to get more wicked, the Lord had a change of heart, at least from what we read in the Scriptures. Perversion and wickedness seemed to be the order of the day in humanity, and God was about to change everything. As a matter of fact, regarding creation, the Scripture says, "for I am sorry that I have made them."

Now, a point of interest is this one: But Noah found grace in the sight of the Lord.

Amid a chaotic situation, the Lord still has His people in touch with Him. There are still those who remain faithful to Him to His cause. My only set of questions are: am I one of those? Would God consider me as one of the faithful? Can He trust me to show up when things matter?

Grace and Favor

The word *grace* means favor. The Lord favored Noah, for Noah feared the Lord God. He esteemed God, and God's values and principles had also become his.

How does a man find grace or favor in the sight of the Lord? What method brings us before His courts and makes us presentable before Him, or at least makes us consider carrying on a task?

Grace and favor are attained by humility in our inward parts. God will always look at a man whose heart is set on pleasing Him.

Another point of interest is this one, where the Lord says, "in the eyes of the Lord."

What does this mean?

For starters, the Hebrew word eyes of the Lord is referenced as an eye. It means from God's perspective or point of view. So, from His viewpoint or point of view, God makes decisions. He looks to see who is humble enough to carry out His wishes.

When God looks at you and me, it is always to see our hearts, not our works or merits. It is always about the soul that is submissive and willing.

As you have seen in many cases, people sometimes give to God out of guilt or serve God out of pity; nevertheless, God is looking for people who understand the calling of surrender and wait before Him with a willing heart.

I don't see how a man can attain God's favor by trying to gain it in any other form but through humility. God won't despise the contriteness of the heart and will perhaps use it as a credential of sorts to qualify a servant for any task.

Under His Shadow Prayer

"May my heart and spirit always be attentive to You, oh Lord. From your point of view, look inside my heart and determine my worth. May I live the contrite life you require and thus qualify me for any given task. Lord, have mercy upon me and use me. Please don't pass me by in my lifetime. May I bring glory and honor to your holy Name!" Amen.

Day 12
The Call to Discipline!

"Now John himself was clothed in camel's hair, with a leather belt around his waist; and his food was locusts and wild honey." (Matthew 3:4)

If there is one thing that I have found to be most helpful both in my walk with God and in the work of ministry, it is the most hated word by the flesh: discipline! As much as people hate the word discipline, it must become fundamental to each of us. You see, discipline is what takes you where you need to be.

I know people have dreams, plans, and ambitions; without discipline, one won't fulfill these things.

After finding or discovering their God-given calling, one should immediately plunge into a life of discipline. This means changing one's lifestyle for the sake of the call, whether it be a ministry, a business, or a vocation.

Discipline is this – bringing one's body under subjection to do what it needs to do to accomplish the task. To not do so is to delay any process in anyone's life. Discipline is the bridge to get us to where we need to be or have been called to be!

Time to Evaluate Oneself!

I have noticed that I have laid a path for discipline in my walk and work. If I want to be successful, I must discipline my life to flow forward in the call. Whether getting up early for personal prayer, bodily exercise, or a reasonable reading time, discipline is necessary. I need this practice to stay caught up in my endeavor.

One of the things we must learn to do is look closely at our mornings and evenings. Are we starting the day preparing for battle; by battle, I mean the tasks that await us. Are we caring for our spirit, soul, and body?

Let me break it down for you:

Our Spirit. This is the spiritual part of us. This is the habitation of God in the Spirit. He lives there. Do we commune with Him? Do we sit at His feet and receive fresh manna from Him?

Our souls include our minds, intellects, and emotions. Are we reading helpful and informative material? Are we meditating to quiet our hearts? Consider this.

Our Body. Are we eating well? Or Are we Fasting? Are we exercising our bodies for better blood flow and energy that will carry us through the day? Consider this.

Under His Shadow Prayer

"Oh, Holy Spirit, don't let me start my days without meeting you for a season of prayer and devotion. Always keep me mindful of the need to discipline me in all areas. Thank you, Jesus, for giving me life this morning. Keep me throughout the day. I love You!" Amen.

Day 13
Baptized!

"When He had been baptized, Jesus came up immediately from the water; and behold, the heavens were opened to Him, and He saw the Spirit of God descending like a dove and alighting upon Him." (Matthew 3:16)

When I first came into the kingdom of God, I would hear pastors and spiritual leaders in my day say, "We need a fresh baptism!" Hearing this, I often thought, I just got baptized; how fresh does the baptism have to be?

They would speak of how a believer needs to be touched by God with His Spirit and His fire. I mean, it was intense, and if you were not walking in God's fire, you would feel less of a servant of God or guilty for not entering it into the flow of God!

As a young convert, my spiritual vocabulary could have been more extensive, and it was hard to understand the language, especially the spiritual one. As I gained more and more understanding of God's things, I realized that the baptism they spoke of was not a baptism in water but a baptism in God's fire. A new touch of God empowered me for the journey, enabling me to discern God's will for my life and the urgency.

Hearing this, I would always ask others who had been believers longer than me, "How do you get this baptism of fire?" To my surprise, not too many could give me answers, for they had never received it.

Then, it happened one day as I met with some brothers for prayer. It was an early morning prayer time when the Holy Spirit came upon me and descended upon me, igniting my heart with His fire and with the evidence of speaking in other tongues. I don't know when it came, but when He did, I knew it! Bless His holy Name!

Let me say that this became my usual way of life. Anything less than a touch of God wouldn't do. I must have Him daily!

This experience was and has been one of the many supernatural encounters I would begin to experience in my walk with God.

When do we need a fresh experience with God? When do we need to be baptized again in God's fervent fire?

You will always know that you need an experience of such proportions when your life is spiritually stale and lukewarm, you feel lost and confused in your walk, or you no longer love Jesus like you used to. These signs say you need a new touch of God in your life.

Baptisms are a symbol of death to self. When you die to that old man, the flesh, called self, then you can now live again in a more refined way as God resurrects you.

Under His Shadow Prayer

"Jesus, touch my heart tonight with your fire; baptize me in your fire and lead me in your way everlasting. You know my anxious heart; please touch me again!" Amen.

Day 14
When God Shuts You In!

"And they went into the ark to Noah, two by two, of all flesh in which is the breath of life. So those that entered, male and female of all flesh, went in as God had commanded him; and the LORD shut him in." (Genesis 7:15, 16)

As I pondered these words in my office this morning, the Spirit of the Lord quickened my heart by saying, "David, when I want to carry out my purposes, I do what I need to do to get full attention from my servants. My urgency is to speak and lead them in the way they should go. Never be surprised by the things I do, and never be confused when I am the One who holds Your life in the palm of My hand."

Being "shut in" sometimes can be puzzling, especially when everything around you seems to be doing well. All the things that are valuable to you, the things that surround you, such as family, friends, work, finances, emotional stability, etc., can be in place, but something inside you says something is not where I need it to be.

When being shut in by the Lord happens in your life, and trust me, if you haven't had this experience yet, you will. When He shuts us in, I experience that you tend to lose your direction and passion, and things become heavy around you. By being heavy, I mean the atmosphere. There is no sense of fluency. Every day is a struggle to get from A to B. You may not understand all I am saying, but I pray God opens your eyes.

I believe God's purposes should be first in our lives. After we do what He wants us to do, we can do what we want, but not before! But in returning to the idea of being shut in, the Lord will often shut you in for a season. It is not to hold you back but to plunge you forward. It is not to lock you in but to align your inward parts with His.

The Holy Spirit will be your guide through this process. He will come and make things around you stale and indifferent. There will be a feeling of almost having no purpose in life; the significance of who you are or what you desire will be gone. It is after this that your desires will begin to align with God. There must be a death to your dreams and ambitions first; then, and only then, can the Lord impregnate you with His heart and mind. Are you ready to be shut in?

Under His Shadow Prayer

"Holy Spirit! My prayer this morning is, please let me walk with You. Show me God's plans for my future. Align all of me with Your will. I want the Father's best for me at this specific time. I don't want to fulfill my earthly dreams, ambitions, goals, or anything that doesn't have Your blessing written on it. Please, God, don't pass me by and lead me." Amen.

Day 15
Don't Buy into It!

"Then the devil took Him up into the holy city, set Him on the pinnacle of the temple, and said to Him, "If You are the Son of God, throw Yourself down. For it is written:
'He shall give His angels charge over you,'
and,
'In their hands, they shall bear you up,
Lest you dash your foot against a stone.'"
Jesus said to him, "It is written again, 'You shall not tempt the LORD your God.'" (Matthew 4:5-7)

This morning's devotion shook me to the core of my spiritual being, and I want to share my findings with you.

The Scripture above is one of the three temptations that Jesus met head-on in the wilderness while He fasted for forty days. I have learned that through fasting, one will encounter some of the most profound, most intense discoveries of the inner battles of humanity.

For one, the self will be exposed, and one will have the opportunity to choose to obey its desires and fall prey to them or follow God's way of escape.

In this one temptation, the Spirit of the Lord showed me an interesting take on this verse.

Taken Up!

"Then the devil took Him up into the holy city, set Him on the pinnacle of the temple...".

As I read this one verse, the Spirit caused me to see the trap of Satan. The devil's strategy is to take us up. Yes, but up where? Up and out of our realm of where God needs us to be.

The flesh is usually frail and tends to be allured to things that make it stand out, seem important, or exalt it to a dimension higher than what God had intended for it to be. This produces pride and arrogance in anyone. No one can handle God's glory and survive it!

The devil took Jesus up; this means higher than God intended for Him to be at this time in His life.

The devil does this without mercy to all humanity. We must know this.

The Battle of the Mind.

Another thing to keep before us is how the devil plays in man's mind. He takes them high and then challenges them to jump off. To throw themselves down, God will carry you and not let you dash your foot against a stone.

This is the lie we tell ourselves when tempted to transgress or in the middle of our sins. We say, " Let me try it; God will carry me if I mess up! "

This must be one of the most wicked traps for any servant of Christ: to believe the devil's lies about doing sinful things and then convince ourselves with the words, " Anyway, if I fail, God will carry me! " If I sound redundant, it is because this is how accurate this truth is.

I am sure you have been to this place countless times.

Don't Tempt the Lord!

Jesus finally quiets the devil and says, "**It is written. Don't**

tempt the Lord Your God." The best defense to this attack is not to entertain it. Always know your sphere where God has put you and listen to the voice of God's Spirit directing you. Tempting the Lord by saying, "I'm going to climb by my own will or desire, and if I fall, the Lord will be there" mentality might not be what you think it is.

I believe the Lord will restore someone who tempts Him, but not before teaching us a lesson that will break us and shatter us to pieces first. Meditate on this.

Under His Shadow Prayer

"Jesus, keep me in Your ways. Give me discernment. Don't let me ever desire to be anything big in my life. Let my lot in life be what You have for me; I want what You want. Keep me in perfect peace as I walk with You daily." Amen.

Day 16
We Are God's Lamp!

"And leaving Nazareth, He came and dwelt in Capernaum, which is by the sea, in the regions of Zebulun and Naphtali, that it might be fulfilled which was spoken by Isaiah the prophet, saying:
"The land of Zebulun and the land of Naphtali,
By the way of the sea, beyond the Jordan,
Galilee of the Gentiles:
The people who sat in darkness have seen a great light,
And upon those who sat in the region and shadow of death
Light has dawned." (Matthew 4:13-16)

How often are we mindful of where we find ourselves? For example, do you consider why God brings people to you that you haven't seen in a long time? You can be at the marketplace, the gym, or the mall, and then suddenly, here comes so and so. Why does this happen?

In other cases, someone you haven't seen in a long while will call you or be looking for you. Do you ever wonder why? It could be an appointed time for you and them! It is never a coincidence with God!

We are God's lamps in the world, called to bring light to the lost. We are called to be an expression of God's glory, a people called to release the fragrance of Christ at work, church, the mission field, family gatherings, etc. Do you see the will of God in us encountering others?

The Bible says that Jesus left Nazareth for Capernaum, to the region of Zebulun and Naphtali. Was Jesus following an earthly manual? A map? A written-out plan from Jehovah God? No. Jesus was following the passion of the Father that had been deposited in Him while He was in glory with Him.

As we walk under the leadership of the Holy Spirit in the purpose of God, we will have an impact on those around us. It doesn't matter who it is or where you go – His glory will be seen from afar! In the case of the people in this region, the Scripture says, **"The people who sat in darkness have seen a great light, and upon those who sat in the region and shadow of death Light has dawned."**

Scripture says that Jesus fulfilled prophecy, which the Prophet Isaiah gave at least 700 years before Christ was born. Jesus wasn't trying to keep this prophetic word; Jesus was living out the Father's will. This is precisely what you and I are called to do!

Under His Shadow Prayer

"Lord Jesus, make my life a fulfillment of prophecy as I follow Your heart here on earth. I hope and pray that those I encounter will experience Your glory and power! I desire to please You and be a testimony of Your goodness to others! As I walk out Your will, make my life count – I don't just want to live out a religion; I want to be Christ to the world!" Amen.

Day 17
The Vision of the Writing Journal!

"And they shall teach my people the difference between the holy and profane and cause them to discern between the unclean and the clean." (Ezekiel 44:23)

Last night, the Lord came to me in a dream and revealed some interesting things to my heart. I want to share this vision with you.

Before I share my dream with you, I need to disclose some things so you can follow it and make sense of it.

I write daily devotions by hand in this specific journal. I own a fountain pen and like to write God's thoughts in my journal in print and cursive style. These journals are costly; they run about forty to fifty dollars each. One thing to note about these journals is that they are leather on the outside and parchment paper on the inside. This particular journal has been out of print since 2020. It is no longer on the market, so when I get a chance, I look for them on eBay and try to purchase them as soon as I find them.

Now to the dream:

As I slept last night, this dream took place around 3 am. Here's what the dream entailed:

About three other people and I stopped at a Walmart. We weren't looking for anything in particular; that is what the dream appeared to show. I noticed a stack of writing journals on the front central aisle. One person with me said, "Look, the journals you have been looking for, and they have stacks of them! "

As you can imagine, I was excited at first glance. Since they have been hard to find, I thought how lucky I was to have found them at Walmart.

As I looked at them on the outside, they seemed identical to the ones I use at home; the outside was leather and outlined in gold trim, and they seemed very nice. I quickly started to put stacks of them in the shopping cart when I suddenly opened one of them and noticed that the paper inside to write on was not parchment but regular 20-lb. glossy paper. I told those who were with me that this was not parchment paper. Take them out of the cart! End of dream.

As I lay on my bed at 3 am pondering what this dream was, I heard the voice of the Lord say to me, "David, you have passed the test of genuineness. You didn't allow yourself to be fooled. You saw the outside of the journal, which seemed real, but when you looked inside, it was false. This is a character trait that all my servants need. To discern the real from the false. Too many buy into the outside or external and never bother to look at the inside of a matter for the truth."

Under His Shadow Prayer

"*Jesus, always open my eyes and ears. I must hear Your voice and see Your glory in all surrounding me. If You are not present, don't let me follow. If You are not speaking, help me discern it. Lead me with Your voice, oh God.*" Amen.

Day 18
The Need to Become Meek!

"Blessed are the meek,
For they shall inherit the earth." (Matthew 5:5)

As Jesus spoke these words, my spirit caught a glimpse of God's heart as He said the words in Matthew 5:5.

We often think God wants to drop an "inheritance" on our laps without a cause; however, the Scriptures teach something very different. Let me share this thought with you if you allow me the time.

Let me start with this insight first. How many times have you wanted to gain access or possess territory but were unable to do so? This has happened to me a few dozen times. I wanted to move forward in the battle but felt powerless. What is the reason that I couldn't overcome it? What hindered me? Was it that I was not prepared for the fight? Was it my lack of faith in God to advance? What has been the real reason for the lack of advancement?

Here's what I have come to realize as I follow my King...

Jesus said something very profound; said, but very deep. He said, **"Blessed are the meek, for they shall inherit the earth."** An inheritance and possession of territory take place, but not for all. Those inheriting anything are a special kind of people; they are the meek!

Let me explain the definition of the word " meek. *Meek* is an adjective that describes a humble, gentle, and mild person. What is truly interesting about a meek person is not that he is recognized as meek; the real key here is how he became meek.

Let's look at it closer.

In a more complete definition, as found in the Greek dictionary, the word meek is someone who becomes gentle through being tamed like an animal. Take the example of a wild stallion. He must be broken before it can be ridden. The same thing happens with people who are rough, rugged, and violent in character. God must break the person down through various tests. Once God accomplishes His purpose in that person – the person becomes useful.

At this time, the person becomes meek and is ready to possess an inheritance. As you can see, this is not a character trait that one is born with but must develop as the servant of God yields to the Holy Spirit's work.

When a builder edifies a house, the foundation must be built with specific details, for the future of that structure depends upon its strength. God always starts working from the inside out. All things in God start this way!

Under His Shadow Prayer

"Holy Spirit, I come to you this early morning with a desire to yield to Your commands. Please show me the path that leads to my inheritance. Meekness is required; I am willing to learn humility to possess what You have prepared for me. Guide me, Holy Spirit, according to Your perfect will." Amen.

Day 19
It's Not About Us!

"And they said, "Come, let us build ourselves a city, and a tower whose top is in the heavens; let us make a name for ourselves..." (Genesis 11:4)

In revisiting and meditating on chapter 11 of Genesis, I came across a familiar passage that was refreshing to my spirit this morning. Let us feast on this beautiful word...

From the families of Noah, some left to the plains of Shinar. These families came to these plains and said to one another, **"Come, let us make bricks and bake them thoroughly."**

When a man or woman of God shuts themselves off to be alone with Him, a creative spirit flows from His throne and releases itself on His children. God will unveil great things to His servants, who will ponder and assimilate the idea He has given them.

Some consider the idea from the Lord, while others quickly

say it's not God! Yet others will say, " Let us pray this idea back to the Lord and see what He leads us to do. " I am a fan of the latter.

In writing this portion, I felt the Holy Spirit releasing some instruction to all of us, His servants.

For some odd reason, I can hear within the words **"Come, let us make bricks and bake them thoroughly,"** the making of a nuclear bomb. It feels that the idea is selfish and carries the power to cause much damage.

We have all had bright ideas that we dared say God gave us. We all have thought of doing many things in the name of the Lord, but deep within, it wasn't about Jesus; it was about us; it was about our reputation, our status, our gain, and our ego being out of control. I believe this was the spirit behind these brick builders.

Just like our temptations, they tend to grow with momentum. Let me share what I mean with you.

We might have an idea, and then someone comes along (possibly one of our closest friends) and says, this is a great idea, a God idea; do it! Their words produce momentum in us, almost as if they give us wings to fly, and we enter the work of the flesh. It looks real, but it is not God – and if we dare to get honest, this is not about Jesus but us!

If we don't heed the Holy Spirit's first warning, we will move to phase two of our carnal dream and say, **"Come, let us build ourselves a city and a tower whose top is in the heavens..."** This is the second step downward.

We start building for ourselves and not God. This is the picture of a servant of God whose proud heart has deceived them. [see Obadiah 1:3]   Even after this, the Holy Spirit may send a messenger to warn us of our selfish project – this is God's mercy.

If we fail to obey, we enter the last phase before some judgment hits us. We say, **"Let us make a name for ourselves..."** No one has this entitlement. Only God's Name is to be exalted and forever adored. This world was not made for the glory of man but for God's Name alone! To Him alone be the glory!

We can see the slow progression downward as we start with a tiny insignificant carnal or fleshly idea and live to see the judgment it brings. We must be mindful always of following

God's heart in all matters.

Under His Shadow Prayer

"Jesus, guard my life with Your Spirit. Don't let me ever do anything not in Your heart for me!" Amen.

Day 20
It's Time to Germinate!

"Foolish man! Don't you know that what you sow in the ground doesn't germinate unless it dies? And what you sow is not the body that will come into being, but the bare seed. And it's hard to tell whether it's wheat or some other seed. But when it dies, God gives it a new form, a body to fulfill his purpose, and he sees to it that each seed gets a new body of its own and becomes the plant he designed it to be." (1 Corinthians 15:36-38 - Amplified Version)

One of my most valuable takeaways from my morning devotion was the word germinate.

In meditating upon the Word of God in my study of 1 Corinthians 15, I discovered what happens when we plant a seed on the ground. For the seed to germinate and take a new form, the naked seed must die- it must go underground and die!

Is it any wonder why there is very little fruit being produced by believers today?

Let us apply this truth to the fundamental discipleship lifestyle.

The John 12:24 Principle!

"Most assuredly, I say to you, unless a grain of wheat falls into the ground and dies, it remains alone, but if it dies, it produces much grain." (John 12:24).

The exciting thing about the Christian walk is that we need to be transformed from glory to glory. God's Spirit leads us this way. As we yield ourselves and surrender our lives more fully to God's Spirit, we are more transformed into His likeness. This is the divine order of the Lord. Unless we are willing to fall to the ground and die, we will be unproductive.

The seed is useless if it remains a seed; it must die to produce a new form with a purpose. Once we understand that God wants to use our lives, but in a refined form, His form and not ours, we will find ourselves a valuable vessel for the Lord. I wholeheartedly believe this is God's will for those who believe.

The Hidden Potential!

Another thing to learn is that no one knows the hidden potential in the seed; only God knows it!

When a seed falls to the ground and dies, it might produce 30-fold, 60-fold, or 100-fold of its original yield. Dying to our old form (as a naked seed) is required [let me add that it must be a willful choice]; resurrecting it to a new, purposeful form is God's work.

Under His Shadow Prayer

"My precious Lord and King Jesus - may my heart always be attentive to the new form you want to bring forth in me. I don't want to block or hinder Your will in my life. Please help me always be conscious of where I am in my spiritual walk. Please let me be attentive to the moving of Your Spirit in me, bringing me ever so aligned with the form You want me to take in every season of my life in You!" Amen.

Day 21
Being Light!

"You are the light of the world. A city that is set on a hill cannot be hidden. Nor do they light a lamp and put it under a basket, but on a lampstand, and it gives light to all who are in the house. Let your light so shine before men, that they may see your good works and glorify your Father in heaven." (Matthew 5:14-16)

My devotion today was a reminder of the heart of God for the lost. I want to thank God first for His word. My heart is just grateful this morning for God's faithfulness towards me. How His word instructs me into action and how His Spirit quickens my mortal flesh unto His service is exceptional. Thank you, Jesus!

Jesus said that we were the light of the world- not just a light but the light of the world. The message that you and I carry within is a message of His glory in the human vessel. We can share this light of God's glory in several ways.

One way to do it is by saying and testifying how Jesus came to make His home in us; another way of giving witness is by living out the nature of Christ in an antichrist world.

Whatever way we choose to be a witness, God must be honored, exalted, and recognized by those who don't know Him or have never met Him. This is what we could call witnessing in its basic form.

Darkness!

The world is dark because of its sin and nature to rebel against its Creator. Darkness always promotes negativity and destruction. John the Apostle said in one of his letters, **"For all that is in the world, the lust of the flesh, and the lust of the eyes, and the pride of life, is not of the Father, but is of the world"** (1 John 2:16).

Until the light comes to the darkness, it will all remain dark. Unless the power of the Holy Spirit converts the human heart, it will remain dark. We must know this.

In Hiding?

Jesus said that the light we carry within must not be hidden.

No one puts a lamp under a bed. Lamps are to lid rooms. So, the call of God upon us is to be light where there is no light. Better yet, discern where there is darkness and light it up!

I know that some of us are bolder than others. Some are shy, timid, or even fearful of the repercussions of what people will say to us for being witnesses to Jesus. Don't let this deter you from the mission God has called us to. I'm sure the devil will try to keep you and me quiet; we must override this thinking with obedience to the mission and not yield the territory because of the lies and fear the enemy brings.

Under His Shadow Prayer

"Holy Spirit, teach me to be bold amid darkness. Help me to be a witness for Your Name's sake. I want people to see the light of Christ in my countenance, my words, and even more, in my deeds. Thank you, Lord, for choosing me to be Your witness for such a time as this!" Amen.

Day 22
Learning to Agree Quickly!

"Therefore, if you bring your gift to the altar, and there remember that your brother has something against you, leave your gift there before the altar, and go your way. First be reconciled to your brother, and then come and offer your gift. Agree with your adversary quickly, while you are on the way with him, lest your adversary deliver you to the judge, the judge hand you over to the officer, and you be thrown into prison. Assuredly, I say to you, you will not get out of there until you have paid the last penny." (Matthew 5:23-26)

One of the great truths this long fast has been birthing in me is learning to agree with my adversary quickly.

Let me explain this powerful truth that the Holy Spirit revealed to me this morning.

The context deals with unforgiveness and offenses. Jesus brings these topics to the surface, as these sins are consequential and will affect not only the person holding on to the offense but also those being blamed for causing it.

I want you to notice how God deals with these issues in the believer's heart. Take note. As the believer comes to worship or spends some quality time in God's presence, the Holy Spirit will arrest his heart and convict him of holding on to an offense or any unforgiveness. This is the best way to heal any offense or unforgiveness, as taught in God's word.

Once asking for forgiveness or reaching peace between both parties occurs, an offering is valuable and acceptable before God. Otherwise, it is only a ritual and not worship.

Agree with Your Adversary!

Who is this adversary? The adversary is the Holy Spirit, who comes to take issue with us for holding on to any offense. He has come to convict you and me; He has come to point His finger at us and tell us what we are hiding inside our hearts. He has come to convict the world of sin, remember?

Jesus says, **"Agree with your adversary quickly while you are on the way with him, lest your adversary deliver you to** the judge, the judge hand you over to the officer, and you be thrown into prison. Assuredly, I say to you, you will not get out of there until you have paid the last penny."

If you have not understood God's heart yet, pay attention: The Holy Spirit has come to convict us of our sins. We must be quick to ask for forgiveness before things get terrible. He will take us to the judge, and then the judge will hand us over to the office, and then we will be put in prison. Can you see this?

Finally, we will not leave the prison until we pay the last penny! In other words, we will enslave ourselves and hurt ourselves in the process, thinking that we are hurting those who hurt us. Let us be wise and listen to the counsel of Jesus, Our Lord!

Under His Shadow Prayer

"Jesus, please help me to see myself in Your light. I don't want to hinder the Holy Spirit in me. I want Him always to direct my steps and quicken me before I end up in prison. I love you this morning, Jesus!" Amen.

Day 23
Beware of the *I Don't Care Attitude!*

" Since all this is true, we ought to pay much closer attention than ever to the truths that we have heard, lest in any way we drift past [them] and slip away. For if the message given through angels [the Law spoken by them to Moses] was authentic and proved sure, and every violation and disobedience received an appropriate (just and adequate) penalty, how shall we escape [appropriate retribution] if we neglect and refuse to pay attention to such a great salvation [as is now offered to us, letting it drift past us forever]." (Hebrews 2:1-3 Amplified Version)

Last night, the Lord gave a vision regarding the condition of our hearts and how disappointment and dark, unpleasant experiences in life have a way of stealing from us the joy and peace that God gives.

In this dream last night, I was talking to an old friend. I haven't seen him in a few years, but it was good to at least have a dream of him and his wife. As I talked to them, I could tell his wife was distraught. It seemed they had been through many disappointments, and now it had carried over to their way of life—end of dream.

A man or a woman can go through challenging experiences in life that one can give up. Absolutely! I have seen this. Others pick up another attitude that says, I don't care anymore!

It is possible to get so discouraged and disappointed that we begin to neglect all that Jesus stands for. Our faith, prayers, trust, and confidence can be put at a place of actual testing.

Seasons of testing come to all, but how we respond to our test determines our maturity and spiritual growth.

The Scripture above says that God's words are genuine and authentic in every way; if we live careless and neglectful lives (being that we have accepted such great salvation from the Lord,) how shall we escape judgment? Others were judged for their unbelief, but what about us who believe? What would be our excuse?

It's time to lift ourselves in the Lord, take ourselves by the neck, and shake ourselves from all the disappointments and discouragements that affect our attitude and undermine our faith in Jesus. We can rise in His Name by pleading the powerful blood of Jesus over our lives and restoring our spiritual life and vitality once again!

Don't give up, soldier! Arise and shine, for your light has come, and the glory of the Lord has risen upon you!

Under His Shadow Prayer

"King Jesus, thank you this morning for the perfect work you have done in me. I know sometimes life seems complicated, and I tend to falter. Yet, in my heart, I know that you will sustain me and enable me to keep on fighting the good fight of faith. I love You, Jesus!" Amen.

Day 24
It's Time to Move!

"Now the LORD had said to Abram:
"Get out of your country,
From your family
And from your father's house,
To a land that I will show you." (Genesis 12:1)

If you have been walking with Jesus for some time, you know that the walk is truly a journey filled with many opportunities for many things. Yet, our walk with God is a walk of purpose and destiny. The Lord is taking us somewhere, though it may sometimes feel like we are stagnant.

This walk with God is indeed a walk of faith; without faith, it will be impossible to know where God is or where God is going. In all sincerity of the word, without faith, we will not be able to please God. I'm sure you have read the Scripture in Hebrews 11.

In our verses above, God had told Abram that he needed to

move and get out of his country, to leave his family and his father's house, for He had a land to show him. At first, the thought of doing something like this would seem extreme. Why should I do this, God? How am I going to do this, God? What is the purpose of this God? I am not living on a simple impulse; there must be more to this invitation, challenge, or dare!

The Lord came to Abram with a plan to unfold His people's future, but Abram didn't know this. How was he to know if his vision was encapsulated only in the sphere of his own family? His only concern was his family and cattle. He had no vision, aspirations, or desire for anything more. Do you see this?

When the Lord came to Abram, he told him about a land he would show him. It was another place, another dimension, yes, another realm. To move here would require very little of his natural understanding; all God was asking from Abram was to have faith and to obey!

Our future destiny will always be based on our obedience to God's words. We must believe what God is saying and take a step. To the flesh, the natural, this kind of move is truly unknown; to the spirit, this move is obvious.

As we endeavor to please God with our lives, let us be attentive to this understanding. I don't believe God considers things the way we do. He is not thinking like us. When the Lord has a plan, He will unveil it to the inner man. He, in turn, provokes all our earthly members to react to it. This is how we get moving in God's direction. Listen to His voice and obey.

Under His Shadow Prayer

"Lord Jesus, I wait upon You for direction. I await Your revelation of what is next in my life. I dare not move to anything that may seem promising or of earthly gain. Come, Lord Jesus, and lead me. I will follow." Amen.

Day 25
Do You Have a Personal Altar?

"...there he built an altar to the LORD and called on the name of the LORD. So, Abram journeyed, going on still toward the South." (Genesis 12:8, 9)

If one thing happens in the heart of the man or woman of God who receives revelation from Him, it is continuing a dialogue with God through prayer. For starters, there is a reason why God talks to His servants, and I dare say that it is due to an ongoing relationship with that servant.

When born again, always look for this sign: an appetite or hunger to be One with Jesus. This is just a reaction deep within anyone touched by God's Spirit. Being hungry for more of Jesus is a natural characteristic, and always look for this in you or those you are helping to grow and mature.

A Life of Prayer

A life of prayer is understanding that God is all and knows

all, and without Him, that servant can't do anything. A prayer life is characterized by the zeal to spend time with God in the morning, throughout the day, and even into the late evenings. This lifestyle is what we call having an altar of prayer.

If you have never disciplined yourself as a servant of the Lord to build an altar of prayer, that holy secret place where you and the Father meet daily, you must try it. It is the most excellent place in your whole house or office.

Abraham heard from the Lord when he was 75 years old and continued to meet God until the day he died. He cultivated this relationship with God even when disobeyed for a season. He knew God had him and would guide him through it all. Abraham trusted God even when nothing seemed to be manifesting.

An altar of prayer will keep us flowing in God's direction even when the emotions aren't present. It is not one of those happy moments for the flesh but a joyous moment for the spirit man.

The man or woman of God must know this one truth: **"Therefore, we do not lose heart. Even though our outward** man is perishing, yet the inward man is being renewed day by day. For our light affliction, which is but for a moment, is working for us a far more exceeding and eternal weight of glory, while we do not look at the things which are seen, but at the things which are not seen. For the things which are seen are temporary, but the things which are not seen are eternal." (2 Corinthians 4:16-18)

If you haven't made a move and built yourself a prayer altar, it might be the time to do so. The faithful servant of God can't afford to live without it!

Under His Shadow Prayer

"Oh, Holy Spirit. You are the One who moves my heart toward God's heart. You always awaken me to pursue God's passion and desire. May my life continually wait upon You for everything- no matter the cost!" Amen.

Day 26
Be Complete!

"Therefore, you shall be perfect, just as your Father in heaven is perfect." (Matthew 5:48)

The old saying, "Nobody is perfect," is a popular saying about those who make a mistake or commit a sin and are called out for it. We have all probably said it at one time or another, but is it correct? Are we trying to prove our innocence using a theological view, or are we only justifying ourselves before those who pointed the finger at us?

Whatever your case, we must be honest about our short-comings and learn to own up to failure when wrong has been committed. The best way to find peace and joy in the Holy Spirit is to yield to His voice and repent when convicted.

Be Perfect!

In the Scriptures above, the Lord Jesus teaches the listener to go above and beyond in all dealings with our fellow man. He says we should do good to others but do it twice. Go the extra mile with the one who asks you to go with him only one mile! Do you get the picture?

As the Lord grows within us, the Holy Spirit will teach us to go the "extra mile." This is God's way of demonstrating true character and nature. The Lord is calling us to go one step further in all things.

What does it mean to be perfect? Jesus said, **"Be perfect just as My Father is perfect."**

Let me show you the definition of perfect as the Greek dictionary defines it: The word perfect means "complete" in compass, with no part outside, nothing that belongs left out.

In other words, to be perfect biblically speaking, one must aspire to be complete and whole. It says with no part outside, not which belongs left out.

One reason we read the Word of God under the direction of the Holy Spirit is to learn God's ways so that we don't leave any part outside and that what belongs to us might be established.

To be perfect is genuinely a challenge. The Bible says to be all you must become in Christ. Pursue it with all your heart to be complete, lacking nothing!

The next time we say, "Nobody is perfect! " Let us examine the word's actual meaning, understand its factual significance, and speak from that perspective. If I am not whole, I must press into it to become whole in Christ.

Under His Shadow Prayer

"Oh! Precious Spirit – make my heart pliable to You. May I be easily broken and rearranged in my own life! I don't want to fight with You because You correct me. I don't want to rebel against Your will at any time. I know that to be complete is work being done in me. Help me be quick to hear and always obey Your voice." Amen.

Day 27
Soaring!

"Surely, in vain, the net is spread in the sight of any bird." (Proverbs 1:17)

To *discern* means to perceive or recognize (something). – *Oxford Languages*

In our walk with God, the journey involves many tests and ups and downs, and the believer must know how to navigate through it all. Strength, wisdom, and understanding are qualities needed as tools to advance toward the mark continually.

With all this said, we need one tool to make our journey more successful –discernment. One must learn how to use this tool to sidestep or jump over any trap set by the enemy of our souls.

You see, trials are made to test our faith, but traps are intended to make us fall with the hope that we never get up again! I know that you have faced both.

Now, the tool of discerning or discernment has, by definition, the ability to perceive or recognize something. This tool is complex human intuition; this tool is given by the Holy Spirit, who has come to lead us in the way.

In the Scripture above, when the enemy lays out a trap, you won't be able to see if you are not flying [like a bird] over a net. The net is only laid out when you are walking in the grass and is almost invisible to the naked eye. No wonder many fall and trip.

Believers are like birds because they have a bird's eye view. Ephesians tells us that the believer has been raised to heavenly places. Read this: **"And you He made alive, who were dead in trespasses and sins, in which you once walked according to the course of this world, according to the prince of the power of the air, the spirit who now works in the sons of disobedience, among whom also we all once conducted ourselves in the lusts of our flesh, fulfilling the desires of the flesh and the mind, and were by nature children of wrath, just as the others. But God, who is rich in mercy, because of His great love with which He loved us, even when we were dead in trespasses, made us alive** together with Christ (by grace you have been saved), and raised us together, and made us sit together in the heavenly places in Christ Jesus...". (Ephesians 2:1-6)

No wonder the word in proverbs says that "in vain, the net is spread in the sight of any bird," because if we are soaring, we will see the trap [net] that the enemy has laid out to trick us.

Under His Shadow Prayer

"Jesus, I can hear Your Spirit moving me through these words. May I always remain in the heavens, soaring as a bird? Give me discernment; open my eyes to see things I can't see; be Lord of my life and lead me in Your ways, oh Lord." Amen.

Day 28
Vision of the Foundation!

"For no other foundation can anyone lay than that which is laid, which is Jesus Christ." (1 Corinthians 3:11)

A couple of nights ago, I had a prophetic dream. Let me share my dream and the vision God allowed me to see.

In this dream, I was at my ministry base, where my office is. I was outside as if waiting for someone to get there with some materials for the building. I had been remodeling our place, restructuring the outside lawn, and re-fencing it. As I waited outside, a lady showed up with a massive tank of water, as big as those carrier trucks that bring fuel to the stores. She parked the car on the side of the road and said, where do you want me to place this tank? I then answered I don't want you to put it on dirt; let me build a concrete slab for it first. It should be ready by tomorrow morning.

As I continued dreaming, I noticed that the bottom of my building had a lot of debris under it. In my heart and mind,

I thought, 'This needs to be removed, and a new foundation needs to be made so the whole building can sit on it!' This was the project that I began to work on.— End of the dream.

Renewal Is Coming!

Renewal is coming to my life and ministry. I genuinely don't know how or when it will happen, but that it is coming is a sure thing! I believe this dream was a call to repentance and allowing Jesus to come and redo my life and ministry and align my destiny for the future.

Undoubtedly, the dream spoke of Christ, my foundation, being laid with a renewed heart. It is not that I need to be born again one more time, but in the dream, it feels like a need to be reconstructed from the inside out, which is an excellent necessity now.

Now, the water tank symbolizes the Holy Spirit coming in more significant measure. The Spirit of God can't be poured out if there is no foundation first. First things first: Jesus must be laid out first, then the Spirit will visit. This is my take on this prophetic dream.

Under His Shadow Prayer

"Jesus, have mercy upon my soul. I pray that I will recognize Your hand at work in my life. Whatever the cost, Jesus, I will pay it. I long to see Your Spirit have His special way in my life. As for the ministry you have given, I will await Your direction. I am in no hurry for anything to happen with it, but I need Your provision and sense of peace upon me. Thank you, Jesus, for always leading my life." Amen.

Day 29
We Need a Fresh Vision of God!

"After these things, the word of the LORD came to Abram in a vision, saying, "Do not be afraid, Abram. I am your shield, your exceedingly great reward." But Abram said, "Lord GOD, what will You give me, seeing I go childless...". (Genesis 15:1, 2a)

This morning, while I was in God's Word, the Spirit of the Lord opened my eyes to see something that touched me deeply. God is always faithful.

As I read the story of Abram and Genesis 15:1, I saw the Lord come to him in a vision and say, **"Do not be afraid, Abram."**

A few things jumped inside of me due to this:

One is that God always knows our concerns, doubts, and fears. So, God was on top of Abram's fear. The second thing I picked up is that the Lord came to reassure Abram that no matter how he felt about his future, it would all be okay.

First Things First!

Can you see how we, like Abram, have the same human tendencies and falter? Abram was good and ready to believe that God had given him a promise a few years back. Since time had come and gone, and there was no manifestation of the promise, he began to worry about his future descendants. He doubted God's promise and more than likely concluded, "This is not going to happen!"

The reason for our failures usually happens when we mistake the spiritual and the natural. All things are birthed in the spirit, then the manifestation happens.

Abram stopped looking at God's face and started looking for His hand. He began to look for the manifestation of the promise and stopped looking at the beauty of God's face!

We will be discouraged when we substitute the inward for an outward manifestation and disappointed if we depend on the outward to keep us happy. It is always about finding joy in the inward; the outward is just the icing on the cake!

God Is More than Enough!

"I am your shield, your exceedingly great reward."

As Abram pondered his future and what he was yet to see manifested, God broke through with a glorious vision of Himself and said, **"I am your shield, your exceedingly great reward."** God didn't tell Abram, "I'm giving you a shield." He told Abram, **"I Am your shield."** Do you see the difference?

We will understand God's wisdom when we learn this language of heaven.

The Lord saw Abram's worry and doubt; however, the Lord helped Abram understand that as great as the promise was, He was greater! He was all Abram needed.

Under His Shadow Prayer

"Oh, my Father, lead me to these living waters. I don't want to ever fall into the trap of materialism. Please save me from believing that life is about things. Life is all about You! May I go deeper into Your heart in this new year!" Amen.

Day 30
Forgive and Set Yourself Free!

"For if you forgive men their trespasses, your heavenly Father will also forgive you. But if you do not forgive men their trespasses, neither will your Father forgive your trespasses." (Matthew 6:14, 15)

We have before us the subject of forgiveness. Should we forgive, or should we not? It all depends on if we want to be truly free. If you allow me, I will show you this truth as the Holy Spirit has opened my heart.

True Forgiveness Is

Forgiveness is a matter of the heart more than an act. If we have an issue with someone who has offended us, we don't have a choice but to forgive them if we want to be free from the bondage of hate, resentfulness, or bitterness.

I know this may not seem fair, but this is what Jesus expects us to do.

Now to the words of Jesus:

The Scripture reads, **"If we forgive men their trespasses, your heavenly Father will also forgive you."** Is this your reading of it?

Think of forgiveness as releasing someone from a prison cell. If we release someone from a prison cell, we will be releasing ourselves from our prison cell. People don't know the power that unforgiveness holds over them when we don't forgive.

Why Hold Anyone Captive?

Some people feel that not forgiving those who have offended them gives them some power over them; nothing could be further from the truth! The one who was offended is continually being damaged emotionally and spiritually.

The Scripture above emphasizes forgiving those who offend or trespass against us. **"But if you do not forgive men their trespasses, neither will your Father forgive them."** This sounds pretty cut and dry to me.

In Dealing with the Offended One

When we are convinced that Jesus is faithful and His word is our final authority, we go the extra mile. Along with forgiving those who have offended us, we pray for them, releasing a blessing over their lives.

Many will say, " Wait a minute! Why should I pray a blessing over them? They are the ones who offended me! "

Remember, unforgiveness puts us in a prison cell. We want to be as far away from this prison as we can. So, make sure that you pray a blessing over your enemies. All because Jesus said so!

Under His Shadow Prayer

"Holy Spirit, take me deeper than ever in my walk with You. I must enter Christ's heart and mind and learn to see things from His perspective. I need to be touched by Your power repeatedly. I desire to walk in Your Word. I know that, at times, I have faltered and broken Your heart. I am sorry for my selfishness and how it dominates me at times. I want to enter forgiveness as You teach us to do so. I don't want to lock myself up in some prison and live the rest of my life in bondage! Have mercy upon me, O God!" Amen.

Day 31
There Will Always Be Two!

"No one can serve two masters; for either he will hate the one and love the other, or else he will be loyal to the one and despise the other. You cannot serve God and mammon." (Matthew 6:24)

The issue of having two masters has been an issue from the beginning of time. There were two trees in the garden of Eden; there were two builders; there were two groups of virgins, the wise and the foolish; there were two roads, a broad and narrow one; and yes, we also have a spirit and a soul.

Why does God bring all these illustrations throughout the Word of God? Why is it vital to understand the battle between the two?

First, let us understand that two is God's way of saying we have a choice. We must choose! We can only have one.

Throughout the Word, the Lord always gives us the one He

wants us to choose. He hints, illustrates, and expounds on the consequences of the good and the bad. This is God's wisdom on display.

He wants us to choose what He desires initially; however, He will wait for us to make our personal choices. This is the kind of God we serve.

Intimacy Is a Key Factor

Our knowledge of Christ has a lot to do with the decisions we will make.

Let me explain further. When we desire to become more intimate with God and enter this life, it will impact our decision-making ability, commitment, and allegiance to Him. When we don't have an intimate walk with the Lord, someone or something else has our attention; yes, this would be the flesh, the soulish part of our lives.

To be governed by the soul (the flesh) is death. Read this: **"For those who live according to the flesh set their minds on the things of the flesh, but those who live according to the Spirit, the things of the Spirit. For to be carnally minded is death, but to be spiritually minded is life and peace."**

(Romans 8:5, 6)

An Unnecessary Battle!

"No one can serve two masters; for either he will hate the one and love the other, or else he will be loyal to the one and despise the other."

The battle of two masters is truly a willful choice. None of us are forced to have this battle; it is one we allow to form when we decide to entertain two masters. We can only please one of the masters at a time.

Now, one master leads to selfishness, which produces corruption, endless pain, and death; the other master has his heart on eternal values. It brings peace and joy to the inward man and produces abundant life in us.

Under His Shadow Prayer

"Jesus, my Lord and King, lead me in righteousness. I desire to please You and only You! Two masters always seek my attention, but know You are my God and Master! Help me always to discern Your Spirit." Amen.

Day 32
What About Life?

"Therefore, I say to you, do not worry about your life...".
(Matthew 6:25)

What an exciting subject the Spirit brought before me this morning. One of the most essential subjects to humanity must be the subject of life.

God has given us life, and how much of it we experience depends on God's timing. As God-created beings, we do our best to be responsible for the life God has so graciously given us; however, our responsibility doesn't guarantee that we will live and breathe here on Earth for as long as we want. Many seem to think so, but I beg to differ.

Let me share what the Holy Spirit showed me this beautiful morning.

In the context above, Jesus teaches the disciples about life and how it can become an idol. If you look closer, Jesus has just finished discussing the impossibility of serving two masters. We could only please one at a time; Jesus referred to God and money as masters.

In the same trend of thought, Jesus clears up the matter of life and how many have become slaves to it.

God Sustains Life

If there is one thing we must realize, God has given us life; this life must be lived out for His glory first and foremost.

This is not the case and can't be the experience of many since they don't know why they were created.

Without Christ in the heart and becoming Lord of it, a person cannot know God's divine purpose.

Is it any wonder why people turn to humanism and invent all kinds of philosophies regarding life- the science of the body, the mind, the soul, etc? Religions are created daily to better oneself and make one's "life" their focus. It's nothing more than a worship of life and not of Jesus Christ the Lord! My friends, this is idolatry!

Do Not Worry!

In Matthew 6, Jesus emphasizes not worrying about life. Why does He say this? I don't believe God condones irresponsibility with life, but I do think He is making a statement about not worshiping life.

You see, life has become a god to so many. They worry night and day about it. They are not free. When something belongs to you, or you make yourself an owner of it, you now must worry about and care for it. This is where it becomes an idol.

If your life belongs to God, He cares and worries about it. He knows everything about this life and how it works; He will supply every need for it. This is a higher level of brokenness in the true disciple of Jesus.

The Gentiles during the times of Jesus didn't know Him as Lord. No wonder they were worried about all the external matters of life. Here is what Jesus said to His followers: **"For your heavenly Father knows that you need all these things. But seek the kingdom of God and His righteousness first, and all these things shall be added to you."** (Matthew 6:32, 33)

We must always seek God first; everything else will be added unto us who believe.

Under His Shadow Prayer

"Jesus, help me to walk in this revelation. I don't want to be consumed with the cares of this world. What I have and don't have must not dominate my life! You must be the One who directs my steps daily! I trust You." Amen.

Day 33
Laughing At God!

"Then Abraham fell on his face and laughed, and said in his heart, "Shall a child be born to a man who is one hundred years old? And shall Sarah, who is ninety years old, bear a child?" (Genesis 17:17)

Have you ever laughed at God? I don't mean laughing as mocking, but because deep in your heart, you didn't believe it was possible. The Bible calls this unbelief. It is unbelief because, in our minds, God can't do or perform a miracle based on common sense or natural science.

Many people have done this quietly. They don't laugh out loud, for somehow, they know better; their fear and doubt sometimes overtake them, and they don't believe.

We have all been at this place at one time or another. We have all felt the inability to make a difference, to change our present situation by mere force, or to take into full consideration our history and make declarations such as, "It will never happen for me!" or "God will do it for someone else, but I'm not worthy!" and the like. You know what I am saying.

Our God in a Box!

You have all heard the saying, Don't put God in a box! This is a ubiquitous expression for those who want to sound spiritual, but the fact is, they are the first ones to do it.

Putting God in a box is a mindset. It is a damning way of looking at life. God is life! He occupies it all. Everywhere we turn, He is there! We can't hide from Him or run from Him. God Is!

Abraham went through something similar. You see, Abraham based everything on the facts at hand. He and his wife, Sarai, weren't supposed to have a child because they were up in age! Naturally speaking, they were not wrong for thinking this.

Part of their minds were set on a limiting factor: they had put God in a box. The other side was that God had shown His faithfulness to them for all these years. So, their challenge was to believe or not believe!

Is it any wonder Abraham laughed at God's words? Consider the facts: anyone would laugh. You see, but herein lies the secret with God. The secret is that those who know Him must believe that God is and that He is a reward to those who diligently seek Him! [see Hebrews 11:6]

Let me add that Hebrews 11:6 must be spiritually understood for it to impact the believer. The spirit within must glimpse God's greatness before faith can be released inwardly!

Under His Shadow Prayer

"Jesus, You said that everything was possible to Him who believed. When I believe You with all that You have given to me, it produces a powerful life-giving force within me. I want to walk continually in this life of faith for the rest of my days. Lead me, Lord; I will follow!" Amen.

Day 34
Spiritual Calisthenics – Part 1

"For physical training is of some value (useful for a little), but godliness (spiritual training) is useful and of value in everything and in every way, for it holds promise for the present life and also for the life which is to come." (1 Timothy 4:8 Amplified Version)

The Spirit of the Lord came to me this morning in a vision and gave me a dream that I would like to share with you. Before I share, I would like you to know that I have been on a protracted fast and I'm about to enter the last week of it, as this will play a role in the dream God gave me this early morning.

My Prophetic Dream

In this dream, I attended a conference outside of my region. It was being held at a church building, where I had never been.

As I arrived and parked my car, I noticed there weren't many people, or at least not yet. As I got out of my car, I looked to my right and saw a lady getting out of her car and getting ready to walk inside. I said to her, *Good morning. Are you here for the conference?* She answered and said, *Yes.* We both made our way inside, and as we entered the church's foyer, I could hear the guest speaker giving instructions inside the sanctuary. So, I made my way inside. Here is what the speaker said: *"Welcome to the conference. So glad you could make it. For the next seven days, we will be studying and doing calisthenics. I will teach you one exercise per day for the next seven days. These exercises will help you stay fit!"* End of dream.

As I pondered the dream in my bed, I heard the Spirit of the Lord quicken me with the interpretation. Here's what the Lord said to me: The calisthenics begin today. I am teaching you seven calisthenics that I consider of high value. If you keep them, you will stay spiritually fit and close to my heart through 2024.

For the next seven days, I will share these spiritual exercises with you as the Spirit of the Lord unfolds.

This calisthenics concerns our faculties (how the human

body receives sensory instructions) of hearing, seeing, touching, tasting, and smelling. Naturally, the body gets instruction this way, but spiritually, our spirit receives revelation in the same way, but in our spirit man.

Spiritual Calisthenic 1: *Spiritual Hearing*

"My dove in the clefts of the rock,
in the hiding places on the mountainside,
show me your face,
let me hear your voice,
for your voice is sweet...". (Song of Solomon 2:14)

The ability to hear His voice is a must for the servant of Jesus. Hearing God's voice and receiving instruction from Him takes some cultivating. Let me show you what I have learned on the subject.

Some needed things are a quiet spirit, the Word of God, and a willingness to be taught.

A quiet spirit is a spirit of humility. That mindset that says, "God is first no matter what!" Secondly, you will need your Bible. Meditate on a small portion of the Scripture, asking yourself, "What is God saying to me?" Finally, be teachable

and always have in your heart to pray this Scripture back:
"Teach me Your way, O LORD; I will walk in Your truth;
Unite my heart to fear Your name." (Psalm 86:11)

Under His Shadow Prayer

*"Jesus, give me a hearing ear. I need to hear Your heart at
all times. Please touch me, Lord, to hear Your sweet voice."*
Amen.

Day 35
Spiritual Calisthenics – Part 2

"[For I always pray to] **the God of our Lord Jesus Christ, the Father of glory, that He may grant you a spirit of wisdom and revelation** [of insight into mysteries and secrets] **in the** [deep and intimate] **knowledge of Him, by having the eyes of your heart flooded with light so that you can know and understand the hope to which He has called you, and how rich is His glorious inheritance in the saints (His set-apart ones), and** [so that you can know and understand] **what is the immeasurable and unlimited and surpassing greatness of His power in and for us who believe...**" (Ephesians 1:17-19 Amplified Version)

Calisthenic 2: *Spiritual Seeing*

The ability to see is our next calisthenic. It has been said that we can only go as far as we see. I agree with this statement. The world follows their own; the believer must follow Christ the Lord. Through His Word, Holy Spirit, and direct revelation to the inner man, the servant of Christ can find His way around this drunken world!

It is not impossible to go wherever the wind blows, but how effective will one be? People often think they are in perfect harmony with God's Spirit simply because they are moving or doing something others approve of. I'm sure you have seen or experienced this. Let me explain further:

When we are led by the Spirit of the Lord, our inner man (our spirit man) picks up the signal and is led to a place with God's approval. This place of approval is what some call God's favor. Who doesn't want God's favor, this blessed place where Jesus smiles at you for your obedience?

When we are led by our desires, ambitions, or goals, we are only pleasing self. Do you see this? The flesh only leads to corruption and, finally, death.

One needs to have a glimpse of what the Lord is doing inside of us and also see how it will affect us externally.

Too many people walk this life trying to improve it by applying principles birthed in self. This usually ends up in some confusion. Until a servant of the Lord learns to see where God is going and follows Him, then and only then can He have and experience true peace within!

Spiritual awareness of God's direction will be critical in the coming months and years. Many are reacting to a cry made in their world. For example, people are moved by politics, science, religion, government, economy, social media, and even people's opinions, etc. Don't let this be you! Walk in the Spirit as you see Him enlightening Your eyes with direction.

Under His Shadow Prayer

"Lord Jesus, open my eyes! I need to see You. I want to follow You with a whole-hearted devotion. Don't let me fall into the enemy's lies and follow his lead. Open the eyes of my heart, Jesus; I want to see You!" Amen.

Day 36
Spiritual Calisthenics – Part 3

"And suddenly, a woman who had a flow of blood for twelve years came from behind and touched the hem of His garment. For she said to herself, "If only I may touch His garment, I shall be made well." (Matthew 9:20, 21)

Calisthenic 3: *Spiritual Touching*

In touching God, I remembered this specific woman reaching out for Jesus. Her issue with the flow of blood and spending all she had to make herself better, but she didn't, stirred her heart for God.

I don't know about you, but touching God involves faith. Every time we reach out to God, we must do so with complete assurance that He is and that He is a Rewarder to those who seek Him!

Calisthenic number 3 concerns touching God. When I speak of touching God, I refer to a touch of faith- a touch that includes an awakened consciousness of God's presence. I believe the woman with the issue of blood had received some impartation from above to touch Jesus as He passed by.

As I share this vision with you, I felt like the Lord was saying, "David, when you touch me, do you do it in faith? Are you expecting anything to happen in you or through you because of Your touch?"

I can think of the many times I have reached out to touch God but with no faith; yes, I had a need, but honestly, I don't believe I've had the faith of God activated. Has this ever happened to you?

The Lord calls me into His heart with faith and full assurance. My touch must be done with faith, the faith of God, not my human faith. We all have human faith, but this is not God's faith; it is not the faith that moves mountains!

As I press into God's heart this season, I desire to touch Him with His faith. As we reach out to touch God, we must never forget that there must be a quickening in our consciousness of Jesus' presence. Without this, our touch is empty; it will go unnoticed by the Lord.

Let us awake and touch Him with the faith He placed inside our spirit-man!

Under His Shadow Prayer

"Today I come before Your holy presence Jesus. I am moved from within; all my inward parts long to be baptized in the fire of Your presence. I ask You to touch my consciousness, awaken my whole being, and make it stand to attention at the sound of Your voice. Also, Jesus, when You are passing by, help recognize and not miss You. I can easily take Your holy Name for granted; I know I have done it many times. Please forgive me for my flippant attitude towards Your holy presence. Oh, how I need a visitation from You, Lord. How my spirit yearns within me. So, in closing my prayer, please hear the cry of my heart; teach me constantly to touch you in faith!" Amen.

Day 37
Spiritual Calisthenics – Part 4

"Oh, taste and see that the LORD is good" (Psalm 34:8)

"May he kiss me with the kisses of his mouth! For your love is better than wine." (Song of Solomon 1:2)

"His words are kisses..." (Song of Solomon 5:16 -The Message)

Calisthenic 4: *Spiritual Tasting.*

The invitation to come before God and taste Him has always been available to all who want more of Jesus. No wonder King David sang about this; He spent countless hours in God's presence, worshipping and expressing his heart before Him.

Let me show you how I have practiced tasting the Lord.

In Song of Solomon 1:2, the precious love story between

Solomon and his lover, the lover says to Solomon, **"Kiss me with the kisses of your mouth!"** Solomon typifies the Lord in this Scripture and invites us to taste his lips and kiss him. You get the picture.

Are You Man Enough to Kiss Him?

God wants us to experience this type of intimacy. You see, not too many want this kind of connection with God, mainly men. Men seem to think that being intimate with God in this manner is not manly!

Remember, in Christ, we are all one before Him: **"For in Christ Jesus you are all sons of God through faith. For as many** [of you] **as were baptized into Christ** [into a spiritual union and communion with Christ, the Anointed One, the Messiah] **have put on (clothed yourselves with) Christ. There is** [now no distinction] **neither Jew nor Greek, there is neither slave nor free, there is not male and female; for you are all one in Christ Jesus. And if you belong to Christ** [are in Him Who is Abraham's Seed], **then you are Abraham's offspring and** [spiritual] **heirs according to promise."** (Galatians 3:26-29)

We Are His Bride!

Let me show you that we, the church, are called the bride of Christ [see Revelation 19:7-9; 21:1, 2]. We are the bride, not the Groom. The relationship between us and Jesus our Lord should be one of intimacy with the One we will spend eternity with.

When the Holy Spirit abides in us, He first shows us God's love for us. As a response, our spirit-man cries from deep within; He expresses Himself by saying, **"Abba Father"** [see Romans 8:15].

In his Knowledge of Word Study, Darrell Bock, *[Bible Knowledge Word Study—Acts through Ephesians. (David C Cook, 2006), p. 179]*, writes that believers may address God with the endearing term (Abba) because he is "our Father," yet (we) should never use this term in the spirit of unsavory familiarity but with the full acknowledgment of his majesty.

My definition of tasting the Lord spiritually is simply this: To taste the Lord is not only to enjoy the revelatory experiences of Scripture but also to experience His immense love, sweet tenderness, and gentle embrace while, at the same time, understanding His majesty and power! Have you tasted the Lord? Have you experienced His kisses? What is your experience of tasting the Lord?

Under His Shadow Prayer

"Oh, my King! I come before You with thanksgiving in my heart and filled with so much gratitude for saving me and putting Your gentle and sweet Spirit within. Lord Jesus, my heart longs for more of Your kisses." Amen.

Day 38
Spiritual Calisthenics – Part 5

Calisthenic 5: *Spiritual Smelling, the Scent of His Presence*

Have you ever experienced the scent of God's glorious presence in your own life? How would one experience this spiritual smell? Can it be done? Is there a unique scent to God and His presence? I believe there is. Let me try to explain.

In researching and smelling God's scent, I discovered that frankincense is one of the primary scents associated with God's presence. In my opinion, it is one of God's most beautiful scents.

In deep times of personal prayer and intercession with God, I have experienced the wonderful scent of His presence: frankincense or myrrh. God knows my heart longs for more of these experiences. You can, too!

The Fragrance of Christ!

Scripture tells us in 2 Corinthians 2:14- 16, **"Now thanks be to God who always leads us in triumph in Christ, and through us diffuses the fragrance of His knowledge in every place. For we are to God the fragrance of Christ among those who are being saved and among those who are perishing. To the one we are the aroma of death leading to death, and to the other the aroma of life leading to life."**

I firmly believe that for a person to diffuse the fragrance of Christ in every place, one must spend time with the fragrant God we serve. As soon as we come into the knowledge of Christ, the fragrance begins to flow.

To add to this fragrance, one must continue in prayer and spend quality time with Him. It is inevitable for a man or woman who spends time with God not to smell or have the scent of God's glory upon them.

In the same way, the sweet incense burned in the Tabernacle and Temple signifies God's presence; we bear the fragrance of God's Presence. We witness our relationship with God through Jesus Christ's victory as an aroma unto life for those who have yet to believe.

I believe that God desires that we develop a more pungent

scent of His glorious presence. Remember, we begin moving in this fragrance when we accept Him into our hearts. Then, we press into Him in prayer and fasting, bringing us to a greater flow of glory before those who don't know Him!

The practice of His presence and His fragrance must be cultivated if we are to have it. The fragrance is present once we begin our journey with Jesus but gets stronger as we intentionally cultivate it and do the things that cause it to flow from us!

Under His Shadow Prayer

"Lord Jesus, take me to this glorious place of more excellent fragrance, where Your life flows unhindered. I desire to testify to Your presence and power; I long to be used by You. Touch Me Oh God! May Your Spirit take me to this place where Your fragrance is so strong that those who don't know You can experience it!" Amen.

Day 39
Spiritual Calisthenics – Part 6

Calisthenic 6: *Exercising the Power of the Faith of God*

"Now in the morning, as they passed by, they saw the fig tree dried up from the roots. And Peter, remembering, said to Him, "Rabbi, look! The fig tree which You cursed has withered away." So, Jesus answered and said to them, "Have faith in God. For assuredly, I say to you, whoever says to this mountain, 'Be removed and be cast into the sea,' and does not doubt in his heart but believes that those things he says will be done, he will have whatever he says. Therefore, I say to you, whatever things you ask when you pray, believe that you receive them, and you will have them." (Mark 11:20-24)

"But without faith, it is impossible to please and be satisfactory to Him. For whoever would come near to God must [necessarily] believe that God exists and that He is the rewarder of those who earnestly and diligently seek Him [out]." (Hebrews 11:6. Amplified Version)

In learning about what God expects me to practice and exercise to position my life for greater fruitfulness, God's genuine faith is another element for me to walk in. Help me recognize the opportunities that You are bringing me this season.

I know that we all have some faith at work in us. Metaphysical faith is the popular one; this is the faith that most Christians attest to having. Yet, this is not the faith that moves mountains. This is a faith that leans on the power of self. This is earthly and will not move mountains; I know this.

The faith that moves mountains is that God imparts to the believer when He is in front of that mountain. This is what some have called real faith.

Real faith is a gift from the Lord for those who ask for it. Does everyone have this kind of faith? The answer is No. Can anyone avail themselves of this real faith? The answer is Yes!

As we ask God for this gift of faith to be manifested in us and through us, situations will present themselves before us where we will need this kind of real faith to make it.

In the Scripture above, the author of Hebrews writes, **"But without faith, it is impossible to please and be satisfactory to Him."** It is obvious to me that in the coming year, God will allow some things to materialize, but only as real faith is exercised.

Get ready to experience God in a fresh way. This year will be a fantastic year to see this happen. Not that it hasn't happened before, but I believe the Spirit of the Lord has noticed this, and my spiritual faculties have caught a glimpse of the immense possibilities of signs and wonders taking place all around me.

Step into this truth of exercising God's genuine faith and start moving in the supernatural.

Under His Shadow Prayer

"Jesus, today I choose to walk in real faith. I know you can do above and beyond anything I can dream of. I believe You impart Yourself into my heart and long to manifest Your power. Lord, I believe this spiritual calisthenic is vital to my spiritual advancement. I want to walk in this power and joy. God, help me realize what You are doing in my life. I yield myself to be taught by Your Spirit in the reality of this faith. Teach me, Lord, I pray!" Amen.

Day 40
Spiritual Calisthenics – Part 7

"While we look not on the things which are seen, but on the things which are not seen for the things which are seen, are temporal: but the things which are not seen, are eternal." (2 Corinthians 4:18) [1599 The Geneva Bible]

Calisthenic 7: Living with Eternal Values in View!

My last calisthenic that I believe the Lord wants me to ponder and genuinely make part of my life is this one regarding eternal values. What does having a perspective of eternal values in view or mind mean? What does this lifestyle entail? I will explain this in this devotion today.

For starters, living with eternal values in mind is a mindset. It's the mindset that says, "Everything you build here on earth will undergo the scrutiny of the judgment seat of Christ. Will it pass the test of fire when it does? For a further study on the Judgment Seat of Christ, read: "**For we must all appear and be revealed as we are before the judgment seat**

of Christ, so that each one may receive [his pay] according to what he has done in the body, whether good or evil
[considering what his purpose and motive have been, and
what he has achieved, been busy with, and given himself
and his attention to accomplishing]." (2 Corinthians 5:10
Amplified Version)

This fire of God will consume our works and our motives.
Nothing will be more searching than God's fire on this day.
So let me outline some things that I believe God will deal
with us about:

Our Worship. Our worship before God will be a thing that
I believe God will see in us. Was our worship done in Spirit
and truth? Did we love God from the heart for who He is,
or were we worshiping God with the selfish interest of what
He could or would do for us?

Our Lifestyle. Was our lifestyle one of true Christlikeness?
Did others see Jesus in us? Was Jesus the One we were living
for? Were every word, thought, and deed done with Christ's
glory in mind? Did we behave before men to make them
want what we had on the inside?

Our Decisions. Did we filter every thought and intent by

passing them through the cross of Christ? Did the Holy Spirit have the right to filter all our desires, plans, and ambitions?

Our Motives. When we acted in the name of Jesus, were we truly and honestly doing it for Jesus, or were we doing it for our gain, status, and gain? Did we try to fool others by saying we were doing something for Jesus when it was for our own ego?

Our Resources. (Time, money, and gifts) Finally, our resources. God has blessed us all abundantly. He has provided for our lives in countless ways. My question is, have we blessed others with what God has given us? Have we paid it forward? God gave us time; do we use our time to bless others? God gave us finances; do we give to the kingdom of God? God has blessed us with talents and gifts; do we use these to glorify and expand His kingdom here on earth?

Consider all these as you journey with God, and with all Your strength, make every effort to please the Father!

Under His Shadow Prayer

"Jesus, as I close my devotion this day, I sincerely pray that

You will always take hold of my hand and lead me. I never want to think I can do this alone or handle situations without You. Jesus lead me; I will follow!" Amen.

Ministry Information

Shabar Publications is a ministry expression under Masterbuilder Ministries, Inc. in Palmhurst, Texas.

This publication ministry, was founded and created for the purpose of writing books and distributing them to the body of Christ both locally and globally.

The intent behind the idea of publishing these works, is to train and equip the reader to be a more intimate lover of Jesus Christ, our Lord!

It is our belief that out of an intimate life with God, by the grace of God, effective ministry will be the outflow.

For more information regarding this ministry, feel free to email us at: mayorga1126@gmail.com.